Original title:
Buttons in the Breeze

Copyright © 2025 Creative Arts Management OÜ
All rights reserved.

Author: Seraphina Caldwell
ISBN HARDBACK: 978-1-80586-150-8
ISBN PAPERBACK: 978-1-80586-622-0

Dancing in the Wind's Embrace

A playful waltz through clumsy hands,
Where mischief twirls on sunny strands.
Clothesline giggles, a fluttering cheer,
As laundry leaps, it disappears!

Heartstrings Tied in Motion

A tangled dance, the threads unite,
With every pull, they take to flight.
Laughter stitched in fabric seams,
Adventures threaded in silly dreams.

The Gentle Pull of Fabric

A tug-of-war with breezy fun,
Where scarves escape like they have won.
Sun hats caper, oh what a sight,
In a playful tussle, they seek the light.

Echoes of a Sewing Circle

With every stitch, a chuckle grows,
As seamstress friends share gossip flows.
Thimbles clink, a joyful sound,
In this sweet chaos, joy abounds.

Airborne Echoes of Color

In the garden where laughter seems to play,
Bright circles dance in a whimsical way.
They flutter and spin like a kite on a string,
Chasing the wind, oh, what joy they bring!

A tumble of colors, they bounce in the sun,
With every small gust, they leap and they run.
They giggle, they twirl in the soft summer air,
To a tune that only they seem to share.

From the porch, my cat stares with wide-open eyes,
As colors collide in a dance that flies.
She chuckles and leaps, trying to catch a few,
But they giggle away, saying, "Not today, you!"

As twilight descends with a wink and a grin,
The echoes of laughter continue to spin.
A festival of hues, oh, what a delight,
In the playful parade of the colorful flight.

Laughter Sewn into the Air

A button flew off, oh what a sight,
It danced with the wind, taking flight.
It twirled round a bird and gave it a scare,
As everyone laughed at the whimsical air.

A cat chased it up, a sight quite absurd,
With a leap and a bound, oh how it stirred.
The button just giggled, so free and so bold,
A story of silliness that never grows old.

Frayed Dreams and Twirling Clouds

In a pocket, a loose thread wants to roam,
Dancing with clouds, it dreams of a home.
A gust whispers jokes, tickling the taut,
While the sky bursts with laughter in a thought.

A hat takes a spin, a sock starts to sway,
As items of laundry join in the play.
Frayed dreams unroll in a colorful swirl,
What a charming show in this fabric-filled world!

The Weight of Laughter

A pin, oh so shiny, began to drop down,
It rolled on the floor, back to the ground.
It tripped on a giggle, then danced past a shoe,
Making all of us laugh, oh what can it do!

Jokes tumble from pockets like loose change in play,
Each chime with a punchline that brightens the day.
With every small jingle, there's joy to unfold,
As laughter weighs lighter than treasures of gold.

Gale's Playful Touch

The breeze, like a jester, pulls at your hair,
Winking at flowers, it doesn't play fair.
A glimpse of a thumbtack, off it will soar,
Chasing down giggles on its playful tour.

It nudges the kite strings in a cheeky tease,
While puffs of soft laughter make hearts feel at ease.
Oh, to be light as a feather and free,
Whirling around with the joy of a spree!

Cascading Traces of the Forgotten

Once in a pocket, now in the air,
Forgotten trinkets dance without a care.
A mismatched sock and an old safety pin,
Claiming the sky, let the games begin.

They tumble and spin, a whimsical show,
Laughing aloud as they shimmer and glow.
Whispers of laundry that flapped on the line,
Now spiraling dreams sipping sunshine wine.

Fabric Leaves in the Sunlight

Tiny fragments flutter, a patchwork of flair,
Splashing the daylight, quite the wild affair.
With each gentle gust, tales begin to weave,
 Giggles erupt as old treasures deceive.

A grandma's old blouse, a pirate's lost hat,
Jive in the sunlight, and oh, look at that!
They twist in the warmth, a playful ballet,
Singing the lullabies of yesterday's play.

The Airy Waltz of Lost Treasures

In a twirl of laughter, they weave and they sway,
Chasing the sunshine, come join in the fray.
Old coins and puffed sleeves, they spin with delight,
A merriment march under skies oh so bright.

Tales of adventure from long ago days,
Resurrected memories sing in a haze.
A button, a feather, a pocketful of jest,
A celebration of life, in the sky they nest.

Dreams Adrift on Soft Whispers

In the gentle zephyrs, whispers abound,
Laughter escapes as they twirl all around.
Invisible charmers on a whimsical spree,
Drifting away, oh where can they be?

A sock with a smile is tumbling down,
While lost bits of joy spin round and around.
With each airy laugh, they knit peace anew,
Drifting on dreams painted in soft sky blue.

Fragments of Heartbeat in the Wind

A playful pitter-patter, oh so sly,
Cascading laughter wonders why.
A polyphonic dance like a tickled kid,
Swirling with glee where secrets hid.

Bouncing around, they skedaddle and hop,
A merry-go-round that will never stop.
Chasing each other like time on a spree,
Whirling through moments, so wild and free.

Soft Murmurs of Adorning Moments

Whispers flutter softly through the air,
A host of giggles that seem to share.
Each tiny jingle, a sprightly tease,
Tickling the mind like a warm summer breeze.

A cheeky grin from a passing kite,
The sun winks back, oh what a sight!
Charming the shadows, with playful grace,
A race of delight in a breezy chase.

Echoes of Charm in the Wild

Laughter rings out as the world spins round,
Each echo a morsel of joy unbound.
They twirl and tangle in the merry air,
A ballet for squirrels, a quest for flair.

Hiccups and hiccups as they bounce along,
The trees laugh too; they hum a song.
Funky and loose, with a hint of sass,
Nature joins in; can't let it pass!

Fleeting Notes of Silence Between

In the lull of whispers, giggles creep,
A secret dance, a playful leap.
They drift on clouds like cotton candy,
Leave a trail of smiles, oh so dandy!

Fluttering echoes in the soft twilight,
Buzzing with mischief, wrapped up tight.
Like a leapfrog game in a twisty maze,
Chasing those moments in a cheerful haze.

Flight of the Colorful Threads

A thread tickled by the sun,
It dances, oh what fun!
With each gust, it takes a leap,
In the air, the colors creep.

The neighbors stare with eyes wide,
At the parade of threads, they ride.
Who knew fabric could explore?
With laughter, they beg for more.

A twist, a turn, a flirty spin,
Looping laughter in the wind.
That cotton's got a mischievous streak,
For fun, it's truly unique.

Atop the hill, they take to flight,
Shimmering under the sunlight.
Every flutter brings a cheer,
Oh, the fabric's joy is clear!

Airborne Chronicles of Fabric

In the park, a fabric crew,
Spinning tales as they flew.
Caught a breeze, and off they went,
On a journey that was meant.

Bright hues shimmering with delight,
They ride the whirlwinds, such a sight.
Stitches giggling in the air,
With twists and twirls, they have a care.

A scarf took off with a wild grin,
Caught in a dance, it wished to win.
A patchwork quilt tried to join the fun,
But ended up tangled, oh what a run!

Each thread's a character with flair,
In the sky, they dance without a care.
With laughter bubbling in the breeze,
It's a fabric fest that aims to please!

Gentle Flickers in the Zephyr

A playful patch upon the lawn,
Floating lightly, it feels reborn.
Whispering secrets on the air,
Threads fluttering without a care.

Tiny stitches start to giggle,
As they twist and turn, they wiggle.
Laughter carried on a tune,
Dancing here beneath the moon.

A ribbon tied to a kite's bright tail,
Soaring high, it tells a tale.
Of fabric with dreams sewn tight,
In the air, they feel just right.

The breeze carries a funny jest,
As they flit about, they jest.
What a sight to see them weave,
In merriment, they won't leave!

Song of the Wind's Whimsy

Listen closely, can you hear?
A symphony that's fun and clear.
Tiny drapes in playful cheer,
Bobbing around as they appear.

A splash of color on a line,
In the breeze, they twist and shine.
Joyful laughter fills the air,
As they float without a care.

A tiny vest on a laughing breeze,
Flirty colors sway with ease.
With a whoosh and a silly twirl,
They dance around in a whirl.

The sun sets low, but they don't dim,
In the twilight, their song's a whim.
Fabric hearts take to the skies,
With each gust, the laughter flies!

Flutters of a Timeless Embrace

Tiny trinkets dance in air,
Laughing softly without a care.
They whirl and twirl with all their might,
In the warm glow of fading light.

A saucy patch from Grandma's quilt,
Flits around, with mischief built.
Tickling noses and grinning wide,
In this playful and joyful ride.

A lost thread, a curious sight,
Tangled up, but feels just right.
Threads of laughter, stitches tight,
Spinning tales in playful flight.

So gather 'round, and let us cheer,
For every flutter we hold dear.
In this moment, let's embrace,
The silly dance, the timeless grace.

Lost Notes in the Breeze

Whispers of melodies on a whim,
Float through air, all loose and slim.
Tickling ears, a funny sound,
A symphony that spins around.

A paper clip, a note once penned,
Laughing loudly, as if a friend.
It soars aloft, so light and free,
In this magical harmony.

Notes from lunch gone astray,
Chasing laughter along the way.
Tickling toes, oh what a tease,
As they flutter upon the breeze.

So let the notes unwind and play,
In this quirky, fun ballet.
For every missed and tangled chance,
Is a tune that begs to dance!

The Harmony of Stitched Wishes

Tangled threads in colors bright,
Spinning tales, a joyful sight.
A wish upon a fabric line,
Dancing under the sun's shine.

A patchwork dream with wavy seams,
Laughing softly, or so it seems.
Each stitch a giggle, each knot a cheer,
Woven with love, and sprinkled here.

Silly patterns prance and sway,
In a fabric world where wishes play.
Stitched so tight, but free to roam,
These little dreams, they feel like home.

So let the fabric lift and glide,
In this grand, whimsical ride.
For every laugh and every hue,
Connects our hearts, just me and you.

Memories Slipping Through Fingers

Fleeting moments on a breeze,
Tickled toes and crumbs of cheese.
Wistful thoughts that slip and slide,
In the laughter, we can't hide.

A sunny day, a sun hat air,
Mischief waits in every hair.
The giggles echo, fit to burst,
As time slips by, we quench our thirst.

Sand between our eager toes,
Drawing circles where laughter grows.
Moments flutter, like butterflies,
As memories dance beneath the skies.

Hold each smile, let the light beam,
In this funny and fleeting dream.
For every laugh, a treasure sings,
As joy around us flaps its wings.

Swaying Wishes Beneath the Sky

When wishes sway like dandelions,
They dance to tunes of sunny time.
With giggles tossed on playful gales,
They flutter high, a joyous climb.

Oh, the hats that spin and twirl,
Chasing clouds, they flip and whirl.
A tug of whimsy on the string,
Bringing laughter, oh what a fling!

Socks mismatched in silly flight,
They wave and wave, a true delight.
Each breeze a chuckle in the park,
As silly shapes ignite the spark.

So let us laugh 'neath open skies,
To twinkling dreams that never die.
For every gust holds secret cheer,
In playful winds that draw us near.

Whimsical Whispers of the Air

In the lightness of soft whispers,
Chirpy giggles ride the breeze.
A kite gets lost in comic antics,
It flaps like crazy, oh what a tease!

Tickled leaves that dance around,
Chase the squirrels, round and round.
Each rustle holds a playful jest,
In nature's scheme, they've passed the test.

A blanket spins, becomes a sail,
Bobbing gently, set to prevail.
With every gust, a secret joke,
The breeze delivers, just like a poke.

So let us join in this parade,
With laughter's shade, the world displayed.
For in the air, where fun runs free,
It's whispers shared, just you and me.

Stories Carried on the Wind

Listen close to tales untold,
Carried softly, brave and bold.
The air brings gossip of the day,
In leaps of laughter, come what may.

A rubber duck floats past a tree,
With silly grins, it's full of glee.
The sunbeam chuckles, casting rays,
As breezy words dance, weave and play.

Raccoons in capes have taken flight,
Plotting mischief under moonlight.
The rustling leaves join in the fun,
A playful breeze, where dreams are spun.

So gather 'round, let spirits flare,
With stories woven everywhere.
For every breeze takes us along,
To lands of laughter, wild and strong.

Wishing for Fleeting Curiosities

A curious hat just took a flight,
Chasing the clouds, oh what a sight!
With every twist and turn it makes,
It beckons wonders, fun, and quakes.

A yoyo spins in unexpected games,
Bringing giggles, from whence it came.
The breeze, a jester, swirls and dives,
In this realm, delight survives.

Silly socks play peek-a-boo,
With every flutter, they're sayin' boo!
Collected wishes glide between,
In endless pranks, the air is keen.

So let us dance with whims anew,
In curious ways, just me and you.
For life unfolds, with laughter bright,
In flying dreams, we find our light.

Tangles in the Open Air

A winding path of thread and lace,
Threads entwined, a comical chase.
A squirrel darts with a curious stare,
While giggles float in the sunny air.

Kites dance high with a twist and twirl,
An eager child gives a joyful whirl.
A mischief-maker, the wind just laughs,
Playing tricks with those tangled staffs.

Stories Written in Thread

In the field, a tale is spun,
Through stitches made in midday sun.
A needle's wink, a crafty peek,
Crafted whims that hide and seek.

Socks debate in playful jest,
Which pair will prove to be the best?
As laughter floats and shadows blend,
The stories swirl, no need to mend.

Revelations of the Wind's Journey

A gusty breeze spills secrets wide,
Through laughter's echoes, joy takes stride.
With every puff, it starts to tease,
Spinning tales with such great ease.

A feathered hat drifts up on high,
Who knows how far it'll fly and glide?
Each flutter sings a silly rhyme,
Wind's revelations, one joke at a time.

The Flight of Fragile Echoes

In the sky, echoes twist and weave,
A dance of sound that won't deceive.
Whispers giggle as they rush by,
Floating on while the clouds roll high.

Can you hear the softest call?
A laugh that bounces, won't let fall.
With every whisper and joyful cheer,
The fragile echoes pull us near.

A Tapestry of Whispered Moments

Tiny treasures dance and sway,
Dreaming dreams of whimsy play.
Caught in laughter's light embrace,
Twirling tales in a vibrant space.

Upon the line we'll hang our hopes,
Each little charm, like joyful slopes.
With a wink, the wind will tease,
Giving chase to giggles, if you please.

Nestled snug on threads of time,
Humor finds its perfect rhyme.
With every flap, a chuckle sings,
Tales of joy that laughter brings.

Bright and bold, they spin around,
In the midst of mirth, profound.
Moments flutter, a jig of cheer,
As each sweet button dance appears.

The Lightness of Unseen Stories

Funky bits in a playful jam,
Sentiments like chocolate ham.
Each a whisper, bright and sly,
Floating 'neath a carefree sky.

Threads of laughter twist and spin,
In the mischief, where joys begin.
Sailing on laughter's tiny masts,
Chasing moments, making casts.

With shy flutters, they drop and rise,
Winking perils, a sweet surprise.
Who knew a breeze could bring such glee?
Grabbing hearts, so wild and free.

A tapestry of giggles sewn,
By hands of fate, a tale well known.
In the lightness, stories thrive,
In the chaos, we come alive.

Soft Emblems of Lingering Joy

Frolicking under a chuckling sun,
Each patch portrays a quirky run.
Whimsical, those fluffs and frays,
Bringing cheer in quirky ways.

Squishy tales on the fabric blend,
Each a giggle, a merry trend.
From pockets deep, the joy spills out,
In twinkling laughs, we scream and shout.

Whirling threads of silly glee,
Painting smiles, can you see?
With every gust, they join the dance,
A merry jig, a sonorous prance.

Echoes of laughter softly cling,
A serenade that makes hearts sing.
In this patchwork of splendid cheer,
Unseen joy whispers near.

Colors Awash on the Whispering Zephyr

Wily hues in a breezy spin,
Each one grinning, daring to grin.
Stitched with laughter, loud and bright,
Canvas of chaos, pure delight.

Swirling tales in the gentle air,
Calm yet chirpy, beyond compare.
Every twirl dares a little quake,
Winds that chuckle, make no mistake.

From pocketed dreams, they flop and splay,
In vibrant strokes, they light the way.
Nudging clouds with a playful shove,
They play along, with hope and love.

In every flutter, a jest's embrace,
In every dash, a merry chase.
Colors rise, a bustling spree,
In the breeze, we're wild and free.

Ballad of the Wandering Ties

In a pocket, lost with flair,
A tie once cared for, now a dare.
It flits about, it twists and twirls,
With knots and loops, it makes us swirl.

Once so crisp, now a wild thing,
It dances 'round like a loose spring.
Catch it quick, or it will flee,
Laughing loud, it shouts with glee.

Poking fun at shirt and vest,
It hides away, it likes a jest.
A fashionable rebel in the scene,
This wandering tie, oh so keen!

Who knew a neckpiece could aspire,
To chase the sun, and dare to tire!
In every breath of silly wind,
A rogue, a prince, a friend to lend.

Interludes of a Forgotten Journey

Once lived a sock, bold and bright,
Chosen for the dance one night.
But it rolled away, seeking fame,
In a land where no socks were the same.

It made companions of stray shoes,
And learned the ways of the traveler's blues.
They giggled as they crossed a stream,
Wet and wild, a tangled dream.

Occasional whiffs of lost cologne,
Together they laughed and called it home.
A sock and shoes on a quest they scheme,
Chasing echoes of a wayward dream.

In corners where dust and dry laughs lie,
They plot escapes beneath the sky.
Unruly paths their pranks ignite,
A journey over day and night.

A Soft Murmur Above

Cracks in the pavement, a story unfolds,
With whispers of wanderers, brave and bold.
An umbrella lost in the flurry of rain,
Hopes and dreams in its fabric maintain.

It hitches rides on the backs of cars,
Giggling softly under the stars.
Slipping through cracks like a wily thief,
It dances on breezes, spreading relief.

Once an accessory, now a wild sprite,
Stitching together the day and the night.
With a wink to the rain and a jibe at the sun,
The soft murmur above has just begun.

Tales of the frolics, the laughter it shares,
Create little snapshots that nobody dares.
With a flick and a dip, into clouds it climbs,
Chasing the moments, collecting the chimes.

A Diaphanous Dance Across Time

A handkerchief sways, in the gentle air,
With a pirouette, it doesn't have care.
Caught in a draft, it drifts on by,
Tickling noses, with a gleeful sigh.

It recalls the past, a pocket of dreams,
Dancing through history, or so it seems.
Wipes away sulking, ignites a grin,
A flag of cheer, waving gently in the din.

From a crumpled jacket to a prince's cloak,
The journey it takes is no simple joke.
Paired with laughter, it lifts the forlorn,
A dance through the ages, silly and worn.

As time twirls on with comical flair,
The fabric whispers of love in the air.
So let it flutter, and spin with glee,
For life's a dance, and so let it be!

Glimpses of a Soft Tether

In the garden of whims, they sway,
Tiny marbles that dance and play.
Caught in laughter, they twirl around,
A silly sight where smiles abound.

With a tug from a playful wind,
A secret game they all rescind.
Flipping like pancakes, they climb high,
Chasing the cloud shaped like a pie.

A knot here, a twist over there,
They launch with flair in the warm air.
Each stitch a giggle, a hairpin bend,
Lively jesters, they never end.

As the sun dips low, they conspire,
To weave a tale of fun and desire.
Snagging dreams in the twilight's glow,
With laughter that only the night can know.

Floating Fancies and Threaded Dreams

A single thread with a grand intent,
Winds through the park without consent.
Whispers of whimsy tugging tight,
To frolic and dance until the night.

Slinking past benches that creak with age,
They chuckle and wiggle, a lively page.
Ropes of delight tied in a knot,
Trails of mischief, called a lot.

A swoosh and a swirl, they take a bow,
Becoming acrobats with every wow.
Under the moonlight, they strut with glee,
Shapes of laughter that no eye can see.

The breeze carries stories, half-spoken laughs,
Of playful schemes and cheeky gaffes.
In a world of color and joy so bright,
They float and flitter into the night.

A Symphony of Loose Ends

In the orchestra of jesters, they play,
Mismatched notes in a delightful way.
Strings of folly, conducting the air,
A melody crafted from silly flair.

Each note a chuckle, each rest a pause,
A rhythm of laughter, without a cause.
When plucked by the sun, they leap and soar,
A concert of fun that we can't ignore.

Around the corners, they trip and spin,
Like carefree sprites, they dance and grin.
Tying loose ends like a twisted verse,
They create a spell that's foolishly diverse.

So let the laughter ripple and flow,
In a symphony of care, let joy grow.
For when they unite in playful embrace,
Life's a sweet tune, a jubilant chase.

Porcelain Smiles in the Wind

Delicate glimmers caught in the light,
Whirling with grace, a comical sight.
Porcelain grins on a carefree ride,
Jubilant faces that swell with pride.

They skitter and scatter, a zany crew,
Poking fun at the clouds while they flew.
With every giggle, they twist and sway,
The essence of joy in an odd ballet.

Draped in soft hues, they gleam and jest,
Silly companions on a whimsical quest.
Chasing the breezes, they sing and laugh,
Enjoying the whims that life may draft.

As twilight wraps them in its embrace,
Porcelain dreams in this silly space.
Unraveled in laughter, they flutter and wink,
A gallery of joy in the twilight's blink.

Swaying Hearts in the Open

On a line they dance and spin,
Each a twirl, a little grin.
Stitching tales in cotton chimes,
Chasing laughter, lost in rhymes.

Tails are fluttering, oh so free,
With every gust they tease the bee.
A charming wobble, a joyful peep,
Swaying hearts in laughter leap.

Who knew seams could come alive?
A playful jig, a carefree jive.
Threads entangled in life's great show,
Chasing whimsy where breezes blow.

In a light-hearted, vibrant race,
Each bright patch finds its rightful place.
With cheerful squeaks and fabric cheer,
Our merry hearts are gathered near.

Threaded Memories Carried Away

A pinball bounce on the clothesline swings,
Old tales woven like curious strings.
Nostalgia crackles in sunny beams,
As laughter threads through childhood dreams.

Old shirts waving like pirate flags,
Chasing birds with their colorful rags.
Each flapping tale is a whispered shout,
"Remember when?" as the breezes pout.

Faded patterns on fabric fade,
But giggles linger in the glade.
Twisted stories of clumsy falls,
Echoing out through memory's halls.

The past flits by in a giggling swirl,
As stitched-up dreams begin to twirl.
In the dance of time, we laugh away,
Threaded joys that refuse to stay.

The Fluttering Fabric of Daydreams

In a breeze, the fabric flies,
Tickling thoughts and sunlit skies.
Colorful swirls on a merry spree,
A playful dance, eternally free.

Every flap tells a hilarious tale,
Of adventurous whims that never stale.
Silliest colors in joyous parade,
Woven wonders that won't ever fade.

From patchwork dreams to wobbly scenes,
Giggles soar like playful machines.
With each gust, a new jest unfurls,
In the fabric of daydreams, laughter twirls.

Forget the worries, let laughter thrive,
As dreams in the sunshine really come alive.
In the fluttering wind, hope will sprout,
With every bright fabric, there's no doubt.

Currents of Forgotten Stitches

Threads of humor on life's great loom,
With stitches forgotten, let joy consume.
In a whirl of winds, they flit and tease,
Woven oddities bring us to our knees.

A bizarre quilt touching hearts with ease,
In every seam, the laughter we seize.
Old mischief folds in fabric divine,
Tangled memories that intertwine.

The freshest stories in old patches,
Chuckling softly as history matches.
Each knot holds a giggle, sewn in delight,
As breezes blow both day and night.

Forgotten stitches weave the past,
In currents of joy, they move so fast.
With a wink of the wind, they start to sway,
Humor drifts softly, come join the play.

The Art of Wind's Caress

In the garden, a gust comes to play,
It dances with leaves, in a jolly ballet.
A hat takes off, with a curious wink,
Chasing its fate, without a blink.

A shirt flutters high, like a flag on a pole,
Spinning and twirling, it loses control.
Laughter erupts from a well-placed shoe,
That tumbles and rolls like it's in on the coup.

Neighbors all chuckle as chaos ensues,
Nature's own antics, everyone views.
A sock joins the fun, it leaps with a twist,
Who knew the outdoors could make such a list?

With ruffles and flaps, the day can't be beat,
In the whimsical world, every flap is a treat.
As the sun sets low, and the laughter recedes,
We wave to the wind, for its playful misdeeds.

Cascading Moments in Motion

A scarf in the sky, it takes its grand flight,
Like a bird on a mission, it catches the light.
Spiders' webs giggle, as they sway on their threads,
While bees gossip softly in their floral beds.

Oh, the mad dance of socks on a line,
Swinging with flair, like they've had too much wine.
A cap does a flip, with a wink and a grin,
Who knew that the laundry could spark such a din?

A breeze brings the laughter; it tickles the trees,
And the fruit on the branches, sways with such ease.
Was that a banana that winked at me there?
In this floaty parade, joy hangs in the air.

So let's gather the giggles and save them with care,
For tomorrow the wind will spread them everywhere.
With moments of motion all filled with delight,
We'll craft a new tale as we laugh through the night.

A Bright Tapestry Unfurled

In fields of color, a wild quilt unfolds,
As the wind plays its tricks, with stories untold.
A wayward petal twirls, just out of reach,
While dandelions whisper, their playful speech.

A napkin goes soaring, a cheeky parade,
As tumble weeds tumble, in comedic charade.
The sun winks at clouds, in a fanciful show,
While butterflies giggle, in the breezy glow.

With ribbons and scraps, the air filled with cheer,
Each twist and each turn, spun from laughter sincere.
A party of colors, on a whimsical thread,
Life's fabric is joyous, where silliness spreads.

As night starts to drift, with a wink and a nudge,
We wrap up the tales, in a bright, cozy smudge.
Tomorrow we'll venture where fun finds its aim,
And create more odd stories, for the wind to reclaim.

The Invisible Thread of Dreams

Through laughter and whims, a journey begins,
Where each silly fluster, feels like it wins.
A lost toy car rolls, on a detour so bold,
Chasing after giggles, through stories of old.

With each gentle breeze, the dreams take their flight,
As shadows make faces, in the soft fading light.
The wind is a friend, with a knack for delight,
Turning worries to winks, in a jolly invite.

A rubber duck sails, on a puddle's great crest,
With a squeaky salute, it appears quite impressed.
Laughter is subtle, stuck on vibrant seams,
In the fabric of fantasy, where nothing redeems.

So hold on to this thread, as you wander and roam,
In this playground of nonsense, we all find our home.
For dreams are like balloons, floating high through the day,
In the invisible threads, we shall giggle and play.

A Dance Unseen by Eyes

A jolly jig on a sunny day,
As fabric twirls in a playful sway.
Whispers squeak in a breezy prance,
A secret party, a merry chance.

Laughter lifts on the warmest gust,
As cloths collide in a joyous thrust.
Tiny claps from the fluttering thread,
A wiggly waltz where no one's led.

Beneath the sky, a hidden show,
With no applause, only a glow.
Colors mingle, a patchwork of fun,
In this breezy dance where all have spun.

So come and watch this lively play,
Where fabric friends come out to sway.
A sight unseen, yet clear in delight,
As the wind giggles, playful and light.

Sketches of Softness in Motion

A canvas wide, with softness drawn,
In gusty frames from dusk till dawn.
Swirls of cotton in a whirl of cheer,
Crafting giggles for all to hear.

Gentle sways paint the air with grace,
As whispers float in a lively race.
Crisp laughter bursts like bubbles anew,
In the softest breeze that coaxes you.

Colors frolic, they skip and tease,
Creating chaos on playful knees.
In sketches made by the winds of mirth,
Each touch a story, of joy and worth.

So grab a seat, feed your curious eyes,
As the wind draws soft, unseen sighs.
In every flutter, in every turn,
A sketch of laughter, for hearts to yearn.

Unseen Threads in the Air

Threads hang loosely, weaving a tale,
Of breezy fables that never fail.
Tickling toes and teasing the breeze,
In threads unseen, where giggles seize.

They shimmy and shake in a gentle dance,
Inviting all to join in the chance.
With a twist and a turn, they play hide and seek,
In a game of whispers, oh so unique.

Through the air, they flutter and flow,
A symphony of laughter, in breezy glow.
Each twist a chuckle, each turn a grin,
Chasing the day, where fun begins.

So let your imagination take a ride,
With threads unseen, let joy be your guide.
Float in the whims, where silliness reigns,
In the playful threads, where laughter remains.

Sails of the Gentle Wind

Sails afloat in a sea of air,
Tilting and turning without a care.
A merry voyage on whimsy's path,
Caught in giggles, embracing the laugh.

Drifting along where the sunshine gleams,
With sails that dance in the sweetest dreams.
They flap and flutter, a colorful sight,
In the arms of the wind, pure delight.

Waves of laughter ripple through the sky,
As sails gather joy, oh my, oh my!
Their journey a loop, a swirl, then a spin,
Carried on laughter, let the fun begin.

So raise your sails in this playful air,
Join the frolic, witnesses rare.
With every gust, in this mirthful tide,
Sails of whimsy, in joy we glide.

Whispers of Color on the Wind

A polka dot flew by my face,
It giggled as it made its race.
A splash of red, a dash of blue,
Spinning tales of joy, it flew.

Breezes tickle, laughter plays,
A riot of hues dances and sways.
With every gust, a chuckle found,
In the silly antics, joy is crowned.

Frilly edges lift with glee,
They're plotting all their tricks with me.
Capes of fabric, grand parade,
As nature hosts a playful charade.

From skies of gray to hues so bright,
Every twirl, a delightful sight.
In the air, a vibrant tune,
As colors dance beneath the moon.

Dances of Fabric and Thread

A patch of plaid whirls with a wink,
Catching the sun, it stops to think.
Cotton swirls and linen leaps,
As the fabric giggles, joy it keeps.

Silks invite a playful glide,
In the gentle wind, they take their stride.
Threads of laughter weave through air,
Stitching moments of fun to share.

Chasing ribbons, laughter spills,
As they bounce through gardens and hills.
Each flicker sings a thread so bold,
In a tapestry of tales retold.

With every fluff, a mischief sought,
In the dance of fabric, I get caught.
A whirl of stitches, laughter's thread,
In this fabric world, we're lightly led.

Echoes of Stitching in the Air

A needle's wink, a thimble's cheer,
With every stitch, a giggle near.
Threads that tangle, twist, and tease,
Whisper secrets in the breeze.

Patchwork jokes, they jump and crack,
As colors burst from the sewing sack.
Each little slip is met with mirth,
In a silly patch of fabric girth.

Frayed edges find a way to roam,
In the wild winds, they call me home.
Echoes of laughter stitch each seam,
As fabric dreams weave into a scheme.

Ticklish threads that pitter-pat,
On dancing feet and fluffy chat.
A cozy quilt of grins displayed,
In every stitch, the fun conveyed.

The Fluttering of Tiny Dreams

A napkin skims across the floor,
Planning adventures, wanting more.
With every gust, it takes a leap,
Into the sky, it dances deep.

Dreams of fabric up in flight,
Fluffy clouds of pure delight.
Colors play, and patterns tease,
As joy flutters on the breeze.

Tiny dreams wrapped tight in thread,
Spinning yarns in your head.
Like jolly sprites, they skip and sway,
In a world where laughter plays.

So let the fabric take its chance,
To twirl and waltz in playful dance.
For every flutter tells a tale,
Of silly moments where dreams prevail.

The Elegance of Tethered Thoughts

A hat with a feather, so grand and so bright,
Twirls with a giggle, takes off in delight.
Then a shoe says, "Hey, come dance with me here,"
While the scarf starts to spin, full of cheer and good beer.

Mismatched and merry, they wander the day,
Chasing each other, in a silly ballet.
Laughter erupts as they jive in a row,
Fashion on a mission, putting on quite a show.

The glove plays the piano, whilst the coat does a reel,
All in good humor, oh, what a surreal deal!
With each gentle gust, they frolic and scheme,
In a world where the ordinary bursts into dream.

And when evening calls, with a wink and a sway,
They gather, exhausted, at end of the play.
A lovely tableau that flutters in grace,
Tethered yet free, in their whimsical chase.

Threads of Joy in Motion

With a flap and a flap, they leap through the air,
Every fabric a dancer, without a care.
The pocket's a joker, whispering puns,
While the bowtie spins tales of outrageous runs.

A curtain of colors, they giggle and glide,
Socks sharing secrets, nowhere to hide.
A dainty lapel pin chuckles and shakes,
Stitches of laughter, oh, what fun it makes!

Fetch me the tidy, the polka-dotted cheer,
Let's frolic in sunshine, no worries, no fear.
With a pirouette here and a jive over there,
Threads of raw joy swirl without a care.

At dusk, they huddle, in twinkling delight,
Offering hugs, as the stars burn bright.
In a patchwork of giggles, the night stretches wide,
While they settle, exhausted, their dreams open wide.

An Untouched Canvas of Air

A breeze kicks up mischief, a twitch of a sleeve,
Chasing laughter and whispers, it dances with leaves.
A fabric of humor, it wraps round the sun,
Creating a canvas where fun has begun.

Tattered balloons float with a giggle or two,
Twisting and turning, like tricks up their shoe.
And oh, a stray napkin, it serves as a clown,
Spinning so fast, it never falls down!

The air is a magician, weaving with ease,
Crafting silliness that hovers like bees.
With each playful whoosh, the world lights a spark,
As joy takes a leap into the wonderful dark.

When the curtain of night draws over the skies,
The chuckles and whispers begin their goodbyes.
Yet the echoes of laughter will conquer the gloom,
In this untouched canvas, where fun still can bloom.

Ebb and Flow of Spirit and Cloth

A wave of old sweaters, the tales that they tell,
Of days filled with laughter, both risen and fell.
A sprinkle of whimsy, stitched tight in the seams,
They dance like the tide, in a sea full of dreams.

The cap's on a journey, till it trips on a shoe,
Bouncing and tumbling with joy that's anew.
The bandana waves proudly, a flag of pure glee,
Join the parade; come along, you'll see!

In swirls and in twirls, the fabric does flow,
Intermingling spirit in a vibrant tableau.
Through sunshine and breezes, they gather and sing,
Oh, the wonderful mess that laughter can bring!

As dusk paints the world in shades of pure gold,
Each thread thinks of stories that never grow old.
Together they whisper, full of joy and mirth,
In the ebb and the flow, they find their true worth.

A Symphony of Textile Whirls

A button danced upon the ground,
With every gust, it twirled around.
It spun and flipped, a sight to see,
A tiny show of pure jamboree.

Amidst the grass, it found a mate,
Together laughing at their fate.
They chased the clouds, so bold, so free,
In this madcap fabric jubilee.

Such jolly games in sunlight's gleam,
The world a sparkling, vibrant dream.
Each stitch a giggle, each thread a cheer,
A patchwork laughter that we hold dear.

Oh, what a whimsical parade,
As humble buttons joyfully played.
A symphony of colors bright,
In every gust, they took to flight.

Gentle Tugs of Nostalgia

A little button from my youth,
Recalls the games, the sweetened truth.
It jingles softly, whispers clear,
Of childhood antics, full of cheer.

With every breeze, it leaps and grins,
In playful sprints, where laughter spins.
A gentle tug, a teasing pull,
Brings back the days that were so full.

Gathered stories in its round embrace,
Of tiny mischiefs, a joyful chase.
It hums along to echoes bright,
In this delightful, breezy light.

A joyful nod to times gone by,
As breezes lift it toward the sky.
With every brush, it sways and rolls,
A dance of memories, tickled souls.

The Chime of Woven Memories

Amidst the breeze, they chime and jingle,
Each button tales that make us tingle.
A youthful spirit in every turn,
To cotton skies, our laughter burns.

They clash and clatter, a melody,
Of antics shared, just you and me.
Each knot and seam, a giggle caught,
In sunshine beams, when life was taught.

A tapestry of joy and cheer,
Woven echoes that draw us near.
As whims of fabric catch the air,
We spin together in gentle flair.

So let the buttons play their song,
In every breeze, we all belong.
A harmony of fun in sight,
With every gust, our hearts take flight.

Threads of Past Adventures

Once a button sailed away,
In laughter's rush, it found its play.
Through fields of green, it took a chance,
To join the wind in merry dance.

Tangled dreams in cotton seams,
Adventures stitched in childhood dreams.
From tiny hands to skies so blue,
A legacy of fun we knew.

Oh, what a journey threads can weave,
In playful spin, we'd never grieve.
Each bounce and skip a tale retold,
Of laughter's spark through days of gold.

So let them roll, those tiny crew,
And chase the winds, on whims anew.
For every gust still calls our name,
In silly games, we're all the same.

Unfolding Dreams in the Open Sky

A paper plane drifts high,
Like a wish thrown to the sun,
Chasing clouds, it twists and flips,
Waving at the morning run.

With laughter caught in cotton tails,
A kite that tumbles, flies so free,
The sky's a playground, wild and bright,
Where hopes can bounce and giggle with glee.

The sunbeams dance on wings of thought,
As dreams take flight from tangled threads,
Each swoop a story, every swirl,
A giggling child, no worries, no dreads.

So here we twirl, in airy glee,
With every gust, our secrets blend,
In the open sky, we learn to play,
Unfolding dreams that never end.

A Palette of Whispers

Colors dance on breezy days,
A splash of laughter, a swirl of fun,
Each hue a giggle, a playful tease,
Catch me if you can, I'm on the run.

Tiny whispers ride the air,
Tickling cheeks like summer rain,
Feathers fly and pencils roll,
All the world's a vibrant game.

Wands of crayons scatter wide,
Riding zephyrs on a spree,
Their tales are painted bright and loud,
In scraps of laughter, wild and free.

So let's create with all our hearts,
A canvas stitched with joy and cheer,
Each brush stroke tells a funny tale,
In whispers that we hold so dear.

Twists and Turns of a Flight

A squirrel darts from tree to tree,
In awkward leaps and funny hops,
Chasing shadows, blotchy trails,
No need for grace when laughter crops.

Airplanes pirouette through clouds,
Stumbling over cotton-fluff,
With winged kerfuffles, a circus in air,
Every loop's a family puff.

A dragonfly does a tango spin,
With missteps that tickle the breeze,
While butterflies share winks and laughs,
In this playful airspace tease.

So let's all join the airborne dance,
With each twist an uproarious sight,
In the sky where the silly play,
Every flight's a chance for delight.

A Breeze of Forgotten Threads

In the air, old stories sway,
From tangled yarns and playful seams,
A breeze carries tales of cheer,
Of woolly teddy bears and dreams.

Nuts and bolts upon a line,
Swinging through with utter grace,
Laughing at the past, they shout,
"Forget the end, it's all a race!"

Rusty zippers in merry spins,
Twirl like dancers lost in song,
Each thread a memory unearthed,
In breezes where we all belong.

So gather round and let us weave,
A tapestry of joyful jest,
With every gust, we laugh and play,
In threads of happiness, we're blessed.

Lightness in the Wind's Embrace

A flutter here, a spin so light,
Unruly dance in the broad daylight.
I chased a loop, it took a flight,
And laughed so hard, what a silly sight!

My hat took off, no warning sign,
Yelled at me, 'Come on, this is divine!'
Off it went, with a twisty whine,
So much for the fashion, it's not so fine!

A paper napkin joined the show,
Waving hello, putting on a glow.
I giggled as it put on a flow,
Pretend it lived, a star of the flow!

Together we pranced, with wild delight,
Giggling at shadows, such a sight.
Every gust brought new **flights of fright**,
In this whimsy, we felt so light!

A Delicate Playlist of Air

Whispers swirl like playful notes,
With each gust, a song that floats.
A cookie wrapper sings and gloats,
While nearby, a lost sock promotes!

The breeze hums in a mischievous way,
It tickles giggles, female and gay.
A chorus of laughter starts to play,
As balloons drift where the children sway!

A napkin waltzes, the star of the show,
With dreams of dance, but where will it go?
Caught in the air, like a maestro in flow,
Conducting the whimsy, stealing the glow!

Each gust brings fresh tunes we adore,
Like popcorn kernels, they pop and soar.
The soft touch of air, never a bore,
Gives life to the laughter, we plead for more!

Encounters with the Unseen

A swirl of mischief dances near,
As a sock slips by, joyous and clear.
It winks at me, oh so sincere,
Making me chuckle, full of cheer!

A leaf takes a tumble, a dramatic flair,
With each gust, a story to share.
It twirls and shouts, 'Life's beyond compare!'
Amused, I join in, without a care!

The wind spins tales of the unseen,
Chasing lost hats, a roguish routine.
In this merry dance, I feel so keen,
To join the adventure, fresh and green!

With each new twist, the laughter blooms,
As objects take flight like hapless plumes.
In this whimsy of nature, joy always looms,
What a delight in the air's funny rooms!

Whimsy of the Wandering Threads

A thread unwinds from a curious coat,
It floats in the air, like a whispering note.
Curled around fingers in a joyous gloat,
What a perfect moment, a sumptuous quote!

Each gust sets it free, in jubilant flight,
Swaying like a dancer, ensnared by light.
It pulls at my heart, a whimsical sight,
I join in the fun, laughing with delight!

A ribbon zips by, on a strong breeze,
Sipping on sunshine, weaving through trees.
It thumbs its nose as if to tease,
Reminding us all to live with ease!

In this playful dance, we share a smile,
Frolicking through moments, worthwhile and worthwhile.

Life's silly threads knit joy all the while,
In the joy of the wind, we find our style!

A Gentle Shift of Past and Present

Little mementos dance and play,
They spin like tops throughout the day.
With every toss, a giggle found,
They twirl and flip without a sound.

Recalling days when life was free,
Where laughter echoed like a spree.
Tiny treasures from yesteryear,
They whisper joy, they bring us cheer.

In a paper chase, they flit away,
Each moment brightens dull dismay.
With every breeze, a shuffling grin,
Rewind the reels, let memories spin.

Fleeting Elegance in the Air

Whispers dance like playful sprites,
Fluttering through the sunny heights.
They tease the silence with a jolt,
A flick, a flap, oh what a bolt!

In gentle gusts, they sway with ease,
A sprinkle of mischief on the breeze.
Like scattered leaves from autumn's care,
They tumble forth, a light affair.

A pirouette, a joyful twirl,
Amidst the laughter, watch them swirl.
With every spin, a tickled heart,
In this lightness, we take part.

The Interlude of a Floating Memory

A soft reminder, a gentle tease,
They soar and dip like playful bees.
In whimsical arcs, they chase the light,
Tickling memories, ever so slight.

With every fold, a story we share,
A giggle escapes into warm air.
They tumble, they twist, a comic show,
Silly and spry, the stars of the flow.

Like the echo of childhood cheers,
They caper, inviting us here.
In a joyful flight, we find our place,
A dance of laughter, a never-ending chase.

Whims of Fabric in the Sun

Dancing fabric in playful sways,
The sunlight catches in fierce arrays.
With giggles sewn into every thread,
They jive and jiggle, joy widespread.

A patchwork quilt, a colorful spree,
Conspiring with breezes, wild and free.
Each twist and flick, a raucous cheer,
In laughter's echo, they're always near.

With merry hues and shades aglow,
They dart and dart, putting on a show.
In the laughter's fold, they find their fun,
A moment's bliss beneath the sun.

The Serenade of Fluttering Emblems

Tiny bits of fabric fly,
Chasing clouds across the sky.
They pirouette with silly grace,
In a dance, they find their place.

With a chuckle and a spin,
They twirl and toss like it's a win.
Bright colors pop and play around,
A carnival of laughs abound.

What a sight, they flutter close,
Wrestling in the breeze, a dose.
Each flap a joke, a playful tease,
As they boogie through the trees.

So let us laugh, let's celebrate,
This parade we can all relate!
For in their whirls, we find delight,
In every twist of this silly flight.

Flutters of Time in the Open Sky

Little snippets swirl and race,
With laughter stitched upon their face.
Time hops like a child's delight,
In the warmth of golden light.

They tumble down like playful charms,
Playing tricks with all their arms.
Some stick close and some drift far,
Oh, how they shine like a falling star!

Each gust brings giggles on the wing,
In this whimsical, joyous fling.
Worn and tattered, bold and bright,
They frolic in the soft daylight.

Oh, to be free, to laugh and play,
As the whimsy leads the way!
When time itself begins to tease,
We soar along with this soft breeze.

Whimsical Notes of Tattered Tales

With a flutter here and there,
Stories ride the balmy air.
Tales of mischief, tales of glee,
Swirling softly near the tree.

Oh, a scrap from Auntie May,
Doing cartwheels in the fray.
Uncle Joe's old patchy cap,
Lands beside a sleeping map.

Each little piece has its own song,
Singing sweetly, all day long.
In the chaos, happiness stands,
As laughter leaps from little hands.

So gather 'round, do not delay,
These stories find their own way.
In a breeze, they spin and weave,
Inviting us all to believe.

The Dance of Adornments in Flight

Adornments launched on playful gales,
   Whirling winks and funny tales.
   Sailing forth with joyous cheer,
   Chasing dreams that disappear.

A bead rolls by, a ribbon glides,
   In this dance, joy confides.
Clinks and clinks with each small turn,
   It's a party for which we yearn.

   Oh, the giggles in the air,
   As they tumble without care.
   Colors burst like tiny stars,
Bringing joy from near and far.

So let the trinkets take their flight,
   As we laugh into the night.
   In this frolic, we all sway,
   In the charm of the merry play.

Patterns Softly Sailing Through Time

A quirky stitch on fabric bright,
Dancing whims in morning light.
They twirl and spin like leaves in flight,
Chasing laughter, out of sight.

With each flap, they tease the day,
Playful friends that love to sway.
In gentle winds, they plot and play,
Creating mischief in their way.

Like tiny sails on sea's embrace,
They map the world with zero grace.
Each gust a comic, wild race,
As they flutter, laugh, and chase.

Through fields of grass and skies so blue,
A merry band, they dance anew.
No need for plans, they'll rendezvous,
In a carousel of joy, just a few.

The Touch of Abandonment in the Open Air.

They drift away without a care,
A playful dance, light as air.
Escaping pockets, oh so rare,
With giggles lost, they shed despair.

Tiny bits that once were snug,
Now levitate, a wiggly hug.
In wind's embrace, a merry tug,
Each moment flips, a silly shrug.

The sun ignites their cheeky show,
They float and frolic, to and fro.
With breezy grins, they steal the glow,
As if to say, we're free to go!

They wave goodbye to hands that cling,
Relishing the joy of spring.
In wide expanses, laughter rings,
And so their freedom, chaos brings.

Whispers of the Fastened

Close companions, stitched with glee,
In corners hidden, they delightfully flee.
Whispers echo in harmony,
A jolly ruckus, wild and free.

In a drawer where secrets lie,
They plan their plots, oh me, oh my!
With mischief glimmering in their eye,
An escape route? Let's give it a try!

Tickling the air, they let loose,
Gyrating dreams, a vibrant spruice.
With every little twist and truce,
They boldly spin, so wild, so profuse.

Under the sun, they flaunt their charm,
In balmy breezes, no cause for alarm.
With flutter and flip, they're free from harm,
Their laughter a captivating balm.

Tides of Unraveled Threads

In tangled threads, a tale unfurls,
They twist and turn, like dervish swirls.
Through loops and knots, pure laughter hurls,
A merry mess of spinning whirls.

With every tug, the stories thrive,
In airy dance, they come alive.
They leap and bound, a joyful jive,
In funny flings, they truly thrive.

Tides of chaos, soft and sweet,
An ocean where all rivals meet.
With every gust, they skip a beat,
Bringing humor to the street.

So let them frolic, let them stray,
In winds of whimsy, come what may!
They play their part in bright ballet,
A spectacle of joy in disarray.

Ephemeral Colors in the Air

A snap and a flip, oh what a sight,
A tumble of hues in the sunlight bright.
They dance like confetti, so full of glee,
Chasing the laughter of a playful spree.

A rogue little knot, oh how it spins,
With giggles and wiggles, it twirls and grins.
The world is a playground, with threads that fly,
Twirling and whirling, oh me, oh my!

A patchwork of dreams, those colors so bold,
In every wild whisper, secrets unfold.
They sway with the breeze, and oh what a tease,
A tapestry stitched with the heart of the trees.

In laughter, they bounce, with no end in sight,
A festival floating, a sheer delight.
Whimsical wonders weave stories anew,
As the sun dips low and the night fades to blue.

The Tide of Colorful Threads

Look at them sail on a whimsical flight,
With each playful gust, they take to the height.
They frolic in patterns, a dainty parade,
Like jesters rejoicing in a colorful charade.

A flick of the wrist, and they scatter like dreams,
Mixed up in mischief, like giggly sunbeams.
Capricious and bright, they giggle and sway,
In this dance with the whims, they happily play.

With jangles and jests that would make you chuckle,
Each twist and each turn is a tickle and buckle.
They pull at your heart with their mischievous charm,
A tide of cuteness, they'll keep you from harm.

They tangle and twist in a colorful whirl,
Each flicker a tickle, a gleeful swirl.
In moments ephemeral, they wish to be seen,
Diving and diving, like a dream in between.

Woven Whimsy in the Air

Up in the sky where the folly is free,
Woven from laughter, how giddy they be!
They giggle and wiggle like fish in a stream,
Creating a canvas, a mischievous dream.

A sprinkle of color, a dash of delight,
They flicker and flounce in the warm, sunny light.
With juvenile glee, they hug every breeze,
Into the great unknown, they dance with such ease.

Their antics are clever, their antics are spry,
They leap and they loll like a jester on high.
Chasing the moments, they twirl with finesse,
A tapestry twisting, oh what a mess!

In the realm of the playful, where giggles collide,
A carnival swirling, where wonders abide.
Each thread tells a story of joy wrapped in air,
Dancing in colors to banish all care.

Journey Beyond the Fabric

Off on a journey where colors unite,
In a world full of laughter, so playful and bright.
They tumble and roll, a brigade of delight,
Through realms of imagination, they take to flight.

Each thread has a tale, with a wink and a nod,
Dipped in a whirl of a leisure applaud.
Like children at play, they frolic with glee,
In this carnival backdrop, wild hearts float free.

They slip through the fingers, they glide and they soar,
A tapestry woven with laughter galore.
Tickled by breezes, they spark like a joke,
In realms of the silly, where laughter awoke.

With giggles and grins, a madcap parade,
In a world made of whims where joy is conveyed.
This journey extends far past mundane seams,
As laughter entwines in the fabric of dreams.

Cascades of Color and Stitch

In gardens bright with stitched delight,
A fabric falls, with colors light.
It twirls and laughs in the sunny rays,
A playful sight that simply sways.

Threads of laughter in the air,
Tickled by whispers, beyond compare.
Each hue a giggle, each stitch a tease,
Woven wonders dance with ease.

As breezes chime, the fabric flares,
Like giggling kids on merry fairs.
With swish and swoosh, they leap and shout,
In joyful chaos, no room for doubt.

So let us skip and twirl about,
Chasing blooms with a playful shout.
For life is but a colorful spree,
A tapestry of humors free.

A Tapestry of Windswept Wishes

A tapestry drapes with a cheeky grin,
Windswept wishes wafting in.
Each longing caught in fabric's hold,
A mischief spun from tales retold.

Laughter catches in every seam,
A fluttering, flapping, whimsical dream.
As the gentle breeze begins to play,
Wishes flit and spin away.

Colors clashing in a merry whirl,
Each twist a giggle, a dance, a twirl.
With every gust, a story unfurls,
A montage of mirth, like graceful pearls.

So let the winds guide our fancies wild,
A patchwork of joy, forever beguiled.
In gusts of laughter, let's sway and drift,
Creating dreams with each playful lift.

Soft Glimmers Amidst the Gales

In gentle gales, soft shimmers play,
Flashes of color dance in the day.
With each flurry, a chuckle escapes,
Winking at clouds that make funny shapes.

The fabric flaps like a kite in flight,
Bringing smiles with every flirty bite.
Glimmers flirt and tease the sky,
A cheerful romp, oh my, oh my!

As whispers twinkle and dry leaves play,
Threads of fun twirl joyously away.
Each step and gust sings a tune so sweet,
A symphony of laughter on the street.

So come, my friend, let's join the fun,
In glimmers bright beneath the sun.
For every moment is a playful tease,
In soft embraces of the friendly breeze.

The Dance of Fabric and Air

In the dance of light and fleeting breeze,
Curtains flutter, inviting ease.
With a skip and a hop, they twirl around,
Like giggling sprites from the ground.

The air chuckles, teasing each fold,
While fabrics whisper secrets bold.
They spin and sway, a spectacle fun,
Dressed in laughter, under the sun.

Patches of whimsy in a vibrant show,
Each pirouette making silly bows.
Life's a merry jig, stitched tight with glee,
In swirls of laughter, wild and free.

So join in the frolic, don't miss the call,
Let your spirit soar, let your laughter fall.
In this fabric waltz, we'll dance till night,
For every breeze holds sheer delight.

www.ingramcontent.com/pod-product-compliance
Lightning Source LLC
Chambersburg PA
CBHW060113230426
43661CB00003B/174